Staff Perspectives

SEXUAL VIOLENCE IN ADULT PRISONS & JAILS

Trends from Focus Group Interviews

MESSAGE FROM THE DIRECTOR

On September 4, 2003, President Bush signed the Prison Rape Elimination Act (PREA) into law. As a part of the law, Congress charged the National Institute of Corrections with a variety of tasks to assist the field of corrections. Included among these are the provision of training and education about the law and the issue which prompted its passage.

A key element of providing this assistance is to build our relevant knowledge about sexual assault in correctional institutions. While it is important to identify and hear from various experts, it is equally important to understand the issue from the perspective of correctional staff. To begin collecting input and information the decision was made early in NIC's PREA Initiative to conduct a series of focus groups at several facilities around the country.

Achieving a regional balance, NIC identified and worked with a variety of prisons and jails, both large and small. Focus groups were conducted with facility executive staff, mid-managers, line officers, and administrative and support staff who perform an array of functions. The participants responded to several questions regarding the problems they encounter in preventing or responding to an incident, and described any successes their agencies had addressing the issue. Questions regarding the dynamics explored what the participants knew generally about sexual assault, plus what procedures had been put in place and what training had been received. These discussions yielded a rich source of information directly from the field about attitudes, knowledge, and current practices.

Staff Perspectives on Sexual Violence in Adult Prisons and Jails: Trends from Focus Group Interviews is an overview of this work and the first volume in a series of bulletins. In addition to key findings, it presents staff views on policy and training, inmate culture, causes and conditions, assault indicators, characteristics of victims and perpetrators, inmate orientation, investigations and prosecutions, and issues regarding responding to sexual violence. It is hoped that these ideas and recommendations will assist you and your agency as you develop strategies to address the problem of sexual violence in correctional institutions.

~ *Morris L. Thigpen, Sr.*

U.S. Department of Justice

NATIONAL INSTITUTE OF CORRECTIONS

Morris L. Thigpen
Director

Larry Solomon
Deputy Director

Dee Halley
NIC Program Manager, PREA

Principal Investigators and Authors

Barbara Owen, Ph.D.

James Wells, Ph.D.

Research Team

Calvin Brown

Yvonne Saunders Brown

Maureen Buell (NIC)

Marianne McNabb

Marcia Morgan, Ph.D.

Barbara Owen, Ph.D.

Diane Schlachter, Ed.D.

James Wells, Ph.D.

Project Director

Anadora (Andie) Moss
President, The Moss Group, Inc.

ACKNOWLEDGEMENTS

As The Moss Group, Inc. began work under a cooperative agreement with the National Institute of Corrections (NIC), our team felt a deep responsibility towards corrections professionals. *Staff Perspectives on Sexual Violence in Adult Prisons and Jails: Trends from Focus Group Interviews*, is the result of a major strategy designed to assess staff perspectives on the dynamics of sexual assault in corrections.

Many persons contributed to this project. At the top of our list is our research team led by Dr. Barbara Owen and Dr. James Wells. The team members were Calvin Brown, Yvonne Saunders Brown, Maureen Buell (NIC), Marianne McNabb, Marcia Morgan, Ph.D., and Diane Schlachter, Ed.D. During a six-month period, members of our team conducted structured focus groups with all levels of correctional staff in adult prisons and jails. We are deeply thankful for their commitment, their willingness to be trained on a rigorous process, and for their patience in recording (verbatim) the comments of staff. We thank the 332 staff who participated in our project and the leadership of their organizations for cooperating so graciously throughout this endeavor.

We would like to give special thanks to Morris Thigpen, Larry Solomon, and Dee Halley for their untiring support for the many aspects of our work and especially their willingness to support an extensive data collection effort. Maureen Buell of NIC was a team member on several of the site visits, and Alan Richardson of the NIC Jails Division was instrumental in numerous ways as we identified locations for the jail site visits.

Finally, thanks to Dr. James Wells, who "crunched" the data; to Dr. Barbara Owen who was the primary author of this work; and to Ania Dobrzanska, who was amazing in her ability to edit the document and push us to a point of completion for this first publication from our data base.

Results from Focus Group Interviews

INTRODUCTION

On September 4, President George W. Bush signed into law the Prison Rape Elimination Act (PREA) of 2003, marking the first time the U.S. government has passed a law to address sexual assault behind bars. Under this Act, the National Institute of Corrections (NIC) is specifically mandated to provide information and assistance to the corrections field in the areas of prevention, investigation, and punishment.

Through a cooperative agreement with (NIC), The Moss Group, Inc. conducted a series of facility focus groups with prison and jail staff concerning their views on sexual assault. These interviews were designed to collect detailed descriptions of staff perspectives on inmate-on-inmate sexual violence in the correctional environment, including knowledge of, and responses to, sexual violence.

Although most respondents discussed male inmate-on-inmate sexual assault, it is important to note that PREA applies to all offenders and staff working with offenders. This focus group was designed to focus primarily on male inmate-on-inmate sexual assault in order to assist NIC to explore this topic in greater detail for the purpose of development of training strategies. While an issue of staff sexual misconduct was mainly mentioned in a discussion about female facilities, staff sexual misconduct happens in all facilities and applies to all staff and offenders.

This bulletin on Staff Perspectives is the first in a series designed to display the wealth of valuable data gathered from the focus groups. Other topics will include investigations, prosecution, women's issues, culture, and jails.

RESEARCH METHOD

Under Cooperative Agreement Number 05S18GJI0, between NIC and The Moss Group, Inc., a series of structured focus group interviews was conducted in 12 jail and prison facilities. The 12 sites were chosen by a purposive sampling method, resulting in a sample that contained large and small prisons and jails, facilities that were located throughout the United States and housed male and female inmates.

A structured protocol, developed by The Moss Group, Inc. was used to conduct the focus group interviews. Using open-ended questions, this protocol elicited staff perspectives on the dynamics of sexual assault, staff knowledge of training and procedures, problems and successes in responding to sexual violence and recommendations for improving this response. Information obtained through the interviews was transcribed and then analyzed using Ethnograph, a qualitative analysis software package.

A total of 332 individuals participated in interviews. About half of all participants were custody staff (27% line staff and 22% supervisors), with executive and non-custody staff making up about one-quarter each. Almost 90% of the participants were employed by a government agency; 65% were male and had been employed in corrections an average of 11 years, with 6 years experience at their current facility. This report describes the general themes observed in these data. Subsequent bulletins will highlight staff perspectives focused on specific critical components important to addressing sexual violence in correctional facilities.

EXECUTIVE SUMMARY

The majority of staff was adamant in stating that they take the problem of sexual violence very seriously. They believed that preventing such violence is part of their job.

Most staff said they had little direct knowledge of incidents of sexual assault. Direct knowledge was gained primarily through reports from victimized inmates, third-party reporters (including other inmates) and participating in investigatory processes.

Many staff felt that they had a sense of when "something was wrong" and said that they could discern potential or actual sexual violence incidents by knowing the inmate population, observing predatory behaviors and potential victims. Staff in all facilities appears to recognize the grooming process and "protective pairing."

Respondents were decidedly mixed on the effectiveness of their institutions' policy, training and overall procedures designed to respond to sexual assaults. Even in the same facility, staff would offer divergent views of existing policy and response protocols.

The difficulty in determining the origin and nature of sexual acts was described as a key issue in responding appropriately to sexual assault.

Across the board, staff believed that sexual assault and other forms of sexual violence were relatively infrequent, but most felt that the actual occurrence was difficult to count.

Challenges staff face in responding to inmate sexual violence included:

- Inmate hesitancy to reporting (including lateness in reporting);
- Making a distinction between coerced and willing sex;
- Inmate's lack of knowledge on how to report;
- Lack of evidence to pursue an investigation;
- Lack of sanctions and punishments for perpetrators;
- False claims by inmates; and
- Prosecutor reluctance to prosecute.

Staff agreed that training on sexual assaults makes prison and jails safer.

In about two-thirds of the facilities visited, staff stated that they had little or no training on sexual assault and other forms of violence. Several reported receiving training on sexual harassment and sexual misconduct, but nothing on inmate-inmate issues. Staff in jails was most likely to receive training on investigations. Staff mentioned the training was often too brief, inappropriate to facility mission, outdated, not targeted to adult learning, presented on a one-time only basis, and noninteractive and non-participatory. Staff from women's facilities stated that sexual assault training typically focused on male-based information and that they received very little information about the dynamics and prevention of sexual assault within female facilities. Many staff from co-gender or female facilities indicated that they had had very little training on working with female inmates in general.

Staff recognized gender differences in causes of sexual assault. Staff stated that male sex drives, forced abstinence, interpersonal conflicts, the exploitative nature of inmate culture, and the pursuit of power over weaker inmates were primary causes of sexual assault. In female facilities, the need to connect with others, histories of abuse and inappropriate sexualization, predatory behavior and staff sexual misconduct were mentioned.

Jail staff was adamant that training and other information resources designed for prisons were often inappropriate for their facilities.

Staff suggested that training should be available to all staff and include information on:

- Agency/facility policy and protocols on responding to sexual assault;
- Staff-inmate rapport, and communication and other issues relevant to reporting;
- An emphasis on prevention of sexual assault;
- Understanding of the process of grooming and protective paring, including coerced and willing relations among inmates;
- Characteristics of predatory and vulnerable inmates;
- Causes and indicators of potential and completed assault;
- Developing sensitivity to inmate victims of assaults;
- Reporting and investigation procedures;
- Services and treatment of sexual assault victims, including crisis intervention training;
- Staff roles and expectations (custody, mental and physical health, investigation, supervisors and others);
- Cross training across the disciplines and functions of the facility;
- Sanctions regarding perpetrators of sexual assault;
- Policy and protocol regarding prosecution; and
- Use of case study and "real world" scenarios.

Staff suggested that forms of inmate education should be held on recurring basis and should include:

- Orientation information at intake/reception; and
- Written materials (pamphlets, posters and the like).

Across the facilities, staff had a fairly consistent view of the characteristics of inmates most likely to be victimized and those most likely to be predatory:

- Vulnerable inmates were more likely to be young, "soft", inexperienced and "weak" mentally and physically; developmentally disabled, and, sex offenders;
- Predatory inmates were likely to be older, have been incarcerated for a longer period of time, and were physically aggressive and "manipulative;" and
- Staff also acknowledged that any inmate could be vulnerable to sexual assault.

Staff identified many issues that compromised the effectiveness of investigations, such as:

- Problems in inmate reporting, changing stories and non-cooperation;
- Difficulties in obtaining physical evidence;
- Inappropriate and uncompassionate approach to inmate interviews;
- Inadequate protocols and lack of training on investigation for all staff;
- Codes of silence (particularly in staff sexual misconduct situations);
- Lack of resources;
- Lack of information regarding the progress of any investigation;
- Use of outside investigators who lack correctional expertise;
- Non-coordination among key stakeholders involved in the process;
- Confidentiality issues; and
- Lack of support by leadership and relevant outside agencies.

Some of the respondents felt that the prosecutor's office was unwilling to aggressively prosecute inmate assault causes.

Staff expressed a concern that PREA requirements could increase the number of false reports and compromise the ability to respond to the legitimate instances.

In every facility, staff stated that staff shortages, design flaws and crowding contributed to sexual violence. Staff coverage was identified as a primary way to prevent sexual assaults.

Staff provided many recommendations for improving the response to sexual assault and other forms of sexual violence:

- Increasing sanctions for inmate predators;
- Elevating penalties for all forms of sexual violence among inmates and sexual misconduct among staff;
- More direct interaction and visibility with inmates;
- Increasing communication with inmates, all staff members and with outside investigators and prosecutors;
- Creating an "after-action review" for all sexual assaults incidents;
- Information on "best practices" in responding to sexual assault;
- Implementing a "safe prisons" officer at every facility;
- Developing a centralized and standardized reporting mechanism;
- Enhancing and publicizing avenues of inmate reporting, including "hotlines," locked suggestion boxes, and outside ombudspersons;
- Improving classification and housing options;
- Creating treatment programs for sex offenders and victims of assault; and
- Use of cameras and other emerging technologies.

SEXUAL VIOLENCE: STAFF PERSPECTIVES ON POLICY

In some facilities, addressing sexual violence was seen as an explicit priority of their overall mission to ensure inmate and staff safety. These facilities had formal policies and protocols created to respond to sexual assault. Training, for staff and inmates, staff positions and prevention, treatment and investigation protocols had been designed to respond to sexual assaults specifically.

In other facilities, controlling sexual violence was an implicit aspect of their mission, but was not named in a specific and identifiable policy or protocol. Most staff agreed that protecting inmates from any form of violence was a critical part of their job. Overall, most participants felt their facility effectively responded to these incidents when the evidence was sufficient to allow formal investigation. Few of these participants, however, reported an emphasis on prevention of sexual violence.

Respondents were decidedly mixed on the effectiveness of their institutions' policy, training and overall procedures designed to respond to sexual assaults. Even with these formal policies, enforcement was uneven for a variety of reasons, including lack of leadership and formal protocols. Some indicated that sexual assault issues were one of the many priorities they were expected to address and was often lost in the shuffle of competing priorities. Even in the same facility, staff would offer divergent views of existing policy and response protocols.

CHANGING ATTITUDES

When I first started 20 years ago and an inmate came out of the cell and told you that he had been sexually assaulted, we told him to get back in there and handle it like a man. I am so ashamed... we were so ignorant then.

Many participants noted that attitudes toward sexual assault of inmates were changing. In the past, many noted, sexual assault was seen as part of "doing time," particularly among male inmates. This attitude appeared to be changing, as described in this comment:

In '96... an offender was lying on top of the table, screaming. He was naked from the waist down. We found two jars of peanut butter inserted in his rectum. This offender was a huge problem for staff and offenders. Most felt he had it coming to him. Later we find that this guy was a molester who had a run in with a family member of his street victim. We were laughing and joking. Now, in this day, that would not be the case. What ignorance we had at that point in time.

Another officer said he was *"glad we are getting away from the attitude that the inmates 'had it coming'."*

INMATE CULTURE

Staff in every facility discussed the role inmate culture plays in sexual violence in prison and jails. Definitions of "weak" and "tough" inmates shape the context of victimization and help explain strong prohibitions against inmates informing on other inmates as well as staff reluctance to intervene to prevent or sanction sexual assault. Inmates are expected to "do their own time" taking by force what they feel they want or need. Male inmates who are seen as weak or feminine are seen as deserving any scorn or abuse they may encounter in their dealings with the strong.

Reluctance to Cooperate

Even when inmates do come forward with a report, complications arise in confirming these reports. The report is often unsupported by physical evidence, witness statements or identification of perpetrators. Victims recanting their original report was also identified as a problem. For example, staff states that inmates do not know how to preserve evidence and may often shower and dispose of clothing or other physical evidence. As one officer explained, "They get rid of this evidence because of their shame (over the assault) and ignorance (of the need to collect data)." It was also commonly stated that even when inmates initially report an assault, they may refuse to submit to a medical exam or recant their statements during the investigation. Often this refusal to cooperate in the investigation is tied to another component of inmate culture: fear of retaliation.

Fear of Retaliation

Staff at all levels agreed that inmates are afraid to report assaults of themselves or other inmates due to their fear of retaliation by the assaultive inmates or other inmates who object to "snitching." Some inmates may be reluctant to report incidents of sexual assault because of shame and guilt, a frequent result of the sexual victimization. In every facility, staff reported that inmates who reported any kind of sexual assault were subject to more violence or at least perceived themselves to be subject to further violence. Even those who present obvious physical evidence of a violent assault are reluctant to admit that they had been victimized; often, alleged victims refuse medical or mental health care. Most systems allow inmates the right to refuse such treatment; in most systems, inmates are not obligated to cooperate with the investigation. Staff suggested that inmates may typically refuse to submit to the "rape kit" or other medical data collection procedures.

False Reports

So where does this start and where does this end? We had an offender popped on the butt with a towel and now he is claiming sexual assault and protection. Inmates will manipulate any system for their own gain.

Officers indicated that inmates will use claims of sexual assault against other inmates that they "don't like;" or "want to get into trouble;" or as "leverage for something else." These false accusations are frustrating to staff because they create additional investigative work on a claim that is difficult to substantiate even when valid.

"Not knowing the validity of inmate stories," was identified as a problem across all facilities. As one member of

an executive team in a jail noted:

The drawback was that there was so much work to check the validity of a complaint. There were so many false positives that there was no faith in the system.

Inmate motivation for reporting presented another dilemma for the officers. As one officer from a very large medium security facility remarked:

Inmates may report that they were assaulted to get out of a cell. It is not easy to distinguish between a real incident and inmate manipulation to gain a cell change, or reporting it to get other inmates in trouble. It is hard to know what is happening in here.

Despite the possibility of false reports, correctional staff acknowledged the harm of sexual assault:

Inmates do have manipulative behavior, but I do not believe that inmates have to be abused here. They are already being punished.

SEXUAL VIOLENCE: CAUSES AND CONDITIONS

Some staff felt that for male inmates interpersonal conflicts, the exploitative nature of inmate culture, the pursuit of power over weaker inmate, sex drives, and forced abstinence, were primary causes of sexual assault. A few staff noted that assault was seen as the only form of sexual release available to inmates. One participant suggested that for inmates who were "raised in jail," the "weak or disgraced inmate" is fair game for sexual exploitation:

The state prisoners are pretty upfront about how they will never have another woman because they are doing life. {Prison sex} is just meeting their needs.

Others felt that most sexual assaults were more about power than sexual gratification. Obtaining sex through "power, control and violence" was a common theme to obtain sex. Some staff viewed the perpetrator as playing mental games to obtain, or exert, power over others. Others stated that it was some inmate's "nature" to extort and take things by force, as suggested by this comment:

Sexual assault has always existed in the penitentiary. We are dealing with a culture in here unlike any culture you see out on the streets. The strong will prey on the weak. New staff isn't prepared for that.

Protective Pairing

The staff interviews point out that some inmates who are afraid of sexual attack may engage in a relationship with one aggressive or high status inmate as a form of protection. Often referred to as protective pairing, staff did agree that much sexual activity is in the form of a shielding relationship between two inmates.

Grooming for Sexual Activities

The act of "grooming" for sexual activity was described in almost every facility. Grooming is a process that involves approaching new inmates with offers of help, and perhaps protection from real or imagined sexual threats from others, with the ultimate aim of creating an obligation for sexual activity. This deliberate process unfolded over time and with little overt pressure and no violence. This grooming process is described here:

Maybe they (new offender) are naïve. They don't have an understanding of what can come about. A scheming inmate will go to a naïve inmate and ask if he needs anything...

During the intake process, new inmates are constantly watched by the more experienced offenders.

Staff also indicated that more sophisticated inmates can identify the predatory inmates and avoid interacting with them. New inmates lack this knowledge.

Housing "somebody that is perceived to be weak and naïve with prison wise inmates" creates a situation where "they will pick out the weak, young kids" and

offer protection from other, more dangerous inmates was also asserted as a problem:

The old offender tells them, 'I am going to watch you and protect you; I will watch your back.' It is a long process. Then the older offender says to the victim, you owe me.' There's also a feeling that if you don't 'give' it, someone might 'take' it. Some inmates get intimidated.

Another participant said:

When inmates are soft; they get tested. [In here], you have to stand your ground within the politics of the facility.
If you do not stand your ground here, you will be victimized. Normally, the players are the guys that have been in the system for a while.

Some respondents suggested that sexual predators may have a personal history of victimization, as conveyed in this remark,

The older predator was a victim in the past. They are now older and more in tune to the prison lifestyle. Yes, they are changing their role. They were the victim and now they are the predator and punishing others for what happened to them. If you are asking about who does it happen to... people are going to be tested, these guys are clueless as to what happens in the jail.

Relational Violence

Many suggested that a large part of sexual victimization was tied to "domestic violence" in both male and female institutions and rooted in relationships that may have begun as consensual and turned coercive over time. These relationships were said to occur among both the "homosexual" inmates as well as those not identified as such. Sexual violence here was defined by the staff participants as a form of domestic violence or "family drama" in male facilities as well as female facilities. This appears to be a challenging dynamic for truly understanding the dynamics of sexual assault.

Consensual vs. Coerced Sexual Relationships

The difficulty in determining the origin and nature of sexual acts was described as a key barrier in responding appropriately to sexual assault. The primary difficulty here centers on distinguishing between consensual and coerced sexual relationships. "One of the hard things about this issue is that one does not want to get involved in a 'lover's spat', but, at the same, time you have to try to take all claims seriously," one manager remarked. He continues by saying that even then "it is hard to determine the real issues — it is not always rape but it always needs to come to custody's attention."

Staff felt that sexual contacts that are initially consensual may devolve into a coerced act for a variety of reasons, such as feelings of shame after the initial act; embarrassment or worry at being discovered by other inmates, feared disapproval by staff or family members; and the discomfort with the behaviors themselves.

Staff may be also unclear as to demarcation line between a consensual act or relationship and a forced or coerced act as covered under the definitions supplied by the PREA legislation, and the more recent Bureau of Justice Statistics (BJS) definitions, state law, and agency policy. This point of view is expressed in this comment:

{While we may} believe that it is consensual sex — not to say that anyone in this institution believes that is OK — but they may be reluctant to report it if it appears to be consensual. Staff may be confused about what is really going on — if there is no {obvious} injury, then is it an obvious rape?

Assaults with violence seemed to be clear cut cases for the staff respondents. But as one person noted, "the consensual act is a totally different issue — it is hard to know about and {thus} hard to respond to."

Homosexual inmates were seen to present a specific problem in making the distinction between consensual and coerced sexual activity, as suggested here:

Take someone with homosexual tendencies. It is hard to tell if they "want it." Maybe they want to be in with the boys {so they engage in sex}. They will be where they can get hit on. It is more difficult (not as obvious) for someone who does not want to be hit on.

The difficulty in distinguishing consensual and coerced acts was also related to inmate reporting issues. As one non-custody staff stated, "It's difficult to determine which claims are real because they won't report it until a month or so after the incident. Also it is hard to know because after they report the incident, a victim will change his mind and (recant) and say it was consensual."

Like everything else in corrections, some issues are perceived to be markedly gendered. Staff in female facilities acknowledged the sexual abuse and trauma histories of their population and its relationship to the issue of prison sex and sexual assault. One staff member in female jail said, "Even if [it] looks consensual, since 80% to 90% of the population has been abused, it's difficult to determine what rape (here) is." Differences in the nature of sexual acts themselves across the genders and the dimensions of prison culture add additional layers of complication, as suggested by this comment:

{Determining coercion} is a big problem... you definitely have to separate. You send them out so they can tell their story... and then one can say "it's just my girlfriend and she was just upset.' Then you are back to where you started... the majority of the females don't have violent tendencies... they don't penetrate someone so we have no proof of an assault.

INDICATORS OF ASSAULT

Physical Signs

Staff reported observing physical signs of harm, such as blood, bruises, black eyes, torn clothes, and other signs of struggle. One staff bluntly suggested that when "I see a black eye, I ask the inmate, 'Who are you blowing?' Another staff said, "{When} there is blood, it is pretty obvious." However, when an inmate reports an assault, the physical signs may not always be visible to the staff. A jail staff person offers this example:

We had a bad situation once. A guy was arrested for a DUI. He came in at night and I didn't see him until the next morning. He said he was raped during the night. I didn't see a damaged anal area on the outside and I could not get a forensic nurse here to examine and to get him to the emergency room. I was very concerned and I felt he could have internal damage.

Behavior Changes

Behavior changes, both social and psychological, were also seen as signs of sexual violence. Staying in a location where staff can easily observe the inmate is one typical indicator that a person has been the victim of sexual violence:

(I recall) a younger Hispanic guy (inmate) who was gay. He did not claim anything; he thought it would be okay. He thought he could handle it, but he was wrong. Four or five guys assaulted him. It was not on our shift, but we found out. He was in the bathroom a lot, going to dayroom, he was avoiding the blind spot.

Psychological signs include behavior changes, such as withdrawal and depression. Suicidal statements and attempts were also discussed, as illustrated in this comment: "I became aware of the rape when I was escorting the victim to the clinic. He had been gang raped. He had slit his wrists and was bleeding."

Other signs of sexual assault include predators following or "staying close" to the potential victim; taking food and other items from their victim; victims withdrawing and becoming quiet; and/or asking to be checked for sexually transmitted disease.

Sex as a Commodity

Sex as a commodity was identified as reality of prison life. In the absence of any other form of support, sex is used by indigent inmates to barter for goods and services within the inmate world or to pay debts. One staff person suggested that when a sex act is "for bartering, then that is not rape...it isn't, but we treat it like a rape case (when reported)."

CHARACTERISTICS OF POTENTIAL INMATE VICITMS AND PREDATORS

Across the facilities, staff had a fairly consistent view of the characteristics of inmates most likely to be victimized and those most likely to be predatory. These factors were true for both male and female offenders. However, many also suggested that any inmate could be subjected to sexual violence, given certain conditions, and those stereotypes about "soft" or "weak" inmates did not always hold true.

Staff identified predictable factors for victims (such as age, appearance, intellectual and mental state, and naivety) described below. However, many staff also suggested that "anyone is vulnerable" in correctional settings and that staff should be aware of other factors beyond these characteristics, as stated here:

There are many risk factors: snitches, younger, newer, and weaker inmates are more vulnerable; but size and stature is not always a strong indicator.

Staff across all facilities indicated that they were aware of these potential vulnerabilities and kept a close watch on those who fit this profile.

The staff offered the following descriptive characteristics:

Age and Appearance

Most staff felt that young male inmates who are small and slight in stature were highly vulnerable to potential victimization. First-time offenders, who exhibited naivety, including lack of criminal or institutional sophistication, were seen as particularly vulnerable. As one participant noted, "The new ones don't know what they are getting into." According to one respondent, predators will "go after the younger inmates, more than the older. Another said that the most likely victim is the "first-time kid that is coming through. These young kids, they don't know. They will be more likely to be taken advantage of than the guy that has been through the system."

"Weak" Inmates

The focus group participants described the impact of the values of inmate culture. Any male inmate who appeared weak by the standards of prison culture and its focus on emotional, physical and mental strength was seen as particularly vulnerable to assault. One participant stated that: "A predator goes after anyone who was weak mentally. They try to fit in and they can't handle it. A guy sees that."

Disabled Inmates

Many focus group participants commented on the vulnerabilities of disables inmates. Predatory inmates will convince the mentally challenged inmates to perform sexual acts by persuasion rather than force. Inmates with diminished mental capacities were said to be unable to "distinguish right from wrong." Eager to please or afraid of higher functioning inmates and incapable of giving consent to any sexual activity, they represented another category of vulnerability. These inmates, "even if the offender is large [in size], if they have the mental capacity of a child, if they have been damaged by drug and alcohol use, they may be slower and easier to exploit."

Again, inability to give consent figures into victimization:

The inmate thought it was consensual, but it was rape. An inmate, who is considered mentally disabled, was actually victimized by another inmate. The staff person thought the victimization was consensual, but didn't factor in the inmate's inability to consent, particularly due to his disability.

Many staff pointed out that jail and prison systems were not designed to manage the significant number of mental health inmates they were now housing.

Housing aggressive inmates and the "mentally challenged inmates" was seen as a problem in many facilities. Even separate housing for at-risk inmates did not solve all the issues. Several focus groups provided descriptions of inmates housed in special units who were subjected to assault by others also housed there. Even when "lower functioning" inmates are housed separately from the general population, one staff reported that "in our chronic needs unit, we don't know what goes on in those rooms when they are closed at night. [Sometimes] a highly functioning person who is sexually active will take advantage of a lower functioning offender."

History of Sexual Abuse

Staff in both female and male facilities also suggested that offenders with histories of prior victimization, either through incest, molestation or other forms of sexual assault, also were more vulnerable to in-custody assault. Staff acknowledged these dynamics were important components in shaping staff training, policy, and practice.

Race and Ethnicity

While some staff suggested that certain racial and ethnic groups were more likely to be assaulted, many participants stated that sexual assault was an intra-racial phenomenon because any attacks across racial lines would upset the delicate racial balance among the inmate groups.

Stigmatization

Staff in male facilities reported that once an inmate had been victimized, he was more likely to be exploited further, as suggested here: "In the yard, inmates get pimped out (if they are known to be victims of rape)."

Feminine Appearance

In male prisons, exhibiting or exaggerating feminine characteristics created potential vulnerabilities. One staff participant commented:

When I worked in the penitentiary, there was a male inmate who was inviting sexual attention in one way or another. He was the most beautiful male who looked like a woman. The other inmates responded and wanted to carry his books, sit next to him, and help with homework.

These feminine appearances were also seen by some staff as more likely to be involved in consensual sex:

When there is an inmate with long hair and looks feminine in people's minds, you don't think that they could be getting raped, and a lot of people believe that it's consensual sex.

Other staff suggested that "feminine demeanor" may also be used as a way to adjust to prison life: "Some guys will do anything to get by. They will offer sexual things to get by, like commissary." Others saw that consenting to sexual acts is the least of two evils, as shown here: "If you're a feminine inmate, you may be better off defending yourself than identifying yourself as scared." In some cases, inmates may choose to align oneself with a stronger inmate as opposed to identifying oneself as scared.

Transgender Issues

Focus group participants described several problems with transgender inmates. Male inmates who identify as female or who have begun the medical sex change process were seen as at-risk for assault by the more sexually aggressive inmates in the population. Some of the participants thought that transgender inmates "invited attention" by their feminine appearance and actively pursued sexual relationships with male inmates.

Homosexual Inmates

While some staff agreed with the view that "homosexuals are bigger targets, as are sex offenders and those with sex offenses against children," others saw that "homosexuals are perpetrators as well as victims." Many respondents suggested that homosexual behavior was also one way that vulnerable inmates survived their incarceration.

Other Forms of Extortion and Exploitation

Staff tied sexual violence to other forms of exploitation. Staff stated that when inmates were victimized sexually, they were also more likely to be exploited in other ways. Reports of sexually victimized inmates giving their assaulter money, clothes, food, commissary items and other commodities appeared in several of the focus groups. Sexual assault was seen by the staff as part of a larger system of exploiting and intimidating more vulnerable inmates.

Sex Offenders

There is animosity against the Chesters (child molesters). The sex offenders have a {particular letter} suffix and everyone knows. The big thing here is child rapists and lots of sex offenders here become victims. They already know how to be a victim, so it's not reported

Participants indicated that sex offenders — particularly those with young victims — were likely to be targeted for assault in a form of "jailhouse justice." Most staff in male facilities described such incidents where known rapists, child molesters and other sex offenders were attacked by other inmates "teaching them a lesson."

Some staff was open about their own negative feelings toward sex offenders, as reflected in this comment: "If it's a baby raper, who would give a s***? Pretty much everyone here doesn't give a s*** about baby rapers." Another staff said, "Everyone has a certain limit... I hate the child molester. First thought is the hell with them, but doesn't still make it {any assault} right." A third comment recognized that "We have to do our job. I don't like to talk to folks that might have molested a child. So I don't look at the charges. I would have a hard time knowing and it would make it more difficult for me, if it was a sexual assault on children."

Characteristics of Predators

Across the focus groups, there was agreement that sexual predators typically were the more sophisticated and aggressive inmates. "Antisocial personalities" and "compulsive sexual behaviors" were other explanations offered in the focus groups. Female staff noted that inmate sexual predators would approach them to "test the waters." Others suggested that sexual predators on the outside (such as rapists and other sex offenders) were likely to be predators in the correctional environment, as illustrated in this comment:

Offenders who commit sexual assault in here are like those who assault women in the free world: [they do it because they are] stronger, [they do it to] degrade and to control.

One participant described the predatory inmate quite simply in stating: "We get tough guys picking on the weak guys and they are afraid." Echoing other comments, one participant said that, "The type of person that is the predator is into power. A lot of times we brush under the table and don't look at it as we should." Another staff person observed that, "Predatory inmates are usually the best programmers; they are often good inmates and don't give you any trouble. They are on their best behavior in front of staff." Predators were often seen to be the more sophisticated "convict," as illustrated here:

{The older offender} was looking at a lot of time. He was a guy that had been through the system. He was a good inmate—he pretty well policed the block for you. He would keep things in line. He pretty well ran the block and kept everyone in line.

In some male facilities, staff also acknowledged the existence of inmate prostitution. Staff said that the sexual assault of a known male prostitute complicated the reporting and investigation. One staff member remarked that, "Prostitution in here isn't rape."

PLACES OF SEXUAL ASSAULT

While some places in jail and prison facilities were seen as more likely for assaults and other forms of sexual violence, most staff participants agreed with the comment that such assaults could occur, "Pretty much anywhere the inmates can go." Typically, isolated areas, "where there is no supervision", and multi-person housing were identified as potential places for assault. In facilities with celled housing configurations, particularly double-celled areas, staff indicated that most assaults took place "in the cells. They don't have a lot of other opportunities here." Other places mentioned in the interviews included unsupervised areas, such as the chapel; showers; dark corners in dorm settings; kitchen and work areas. As one person suggested, "They will hunt out spots, they won't be seen. Showers, rest rooms and living units were most often mentioned in female facilities."

STAFF RESPONDING
TO SEXUAL VIOLENCE

I wish we had a way to protect the inmates. That is my job and if we can't protect them, what is the point? That is my biggest problem — for them to trust us without repercussions. We need more of a presence for us to feel like we can protect them and they can trust us. We have too many criminals and not enough staff.

The focus groups participants described multiple difficulties in responding to sexual violence:

- Elements of inmate culture that supports exploitation of "weak", "soft" and vulnerable inmates;

- Inmate resistance to reporting (including lack of trust, untimely reporting, shame and humiliation, and fear of retaliation and re-victimization);

- Making a distinction between coerced and consensual sex;

- Inmate's lack of knowledge on how to report;

- Lack of evidence to pursue an investigation;

- Lack of sanctions and punishments for perpetrators;

- False claims and manipulation by inmates; and

- Prosecutor reluctance to prosecute.

The difficulty of responding was described by this respondent:

{We respond to every assault situation}... however with rape we don't always know the situation so it's difficult to respond {when we don't have all the information}. When we get the information, we act on it and take appropriate measures. We respond well when we know about the situation, but with assault, {we don't always know all the facts}.

There was also some discussion of the dampening effect of the patient confidentiality laws when inmates report assaults to medical or mental health personnel. Many of the mental health and counseling staff participating in the focus group interviews stated that they could not report anything inmates told them during counseling or therapy sessions without express permission from the inmate. Often, inmates wanted to disclose the event and sought help for their trauma, but were unwilling to pursue formal investigation channels. Custody staff, in turn, expressed frustration at this process. Other first-respondents noted the difficulty in obtaining any follow up information where investigations were deemed confidential.

One issue involves keeping information about an assault and its investigation confidential, both in order to protect the victim and to protect the integrity of the investigation. Line officers sometimes expressed frustration that confidentiality issues prohibited receiving information about an incident after the report "went up the ladder." Other officers suggested that "everyone knows everything" in an institution, including inmates, so confidentiality was not a problem. If rumors start, that tells other inmates not to trust us and not to report it. I don't know how confidentiality (the process) needs to be stressed more."

Jail and prison staff pointed out that they lacked a private space to interview inmates and acknowledged the problems involved in "pulling an inmate out" of a housing unit for these conversations. Calling an inmate out of the housing unit creates suspicion that he or she may be "snitching" and may create further risk for the inmate. One counselor explained that her office was separated by partitions that allowed sound to travel, and said, "I am afraid that other inmates will hear what the inmate is saying. That makes it hard for him to give up his enemy's name."

Many staff expressed the desire to develop inmate trust, specifically around the extremely sensitive topic of sexual assault between males, as reflected in this comment:

We have to get past the stereotype (held by inmates) that when you come to an officer and report a problem, you are going to be told to go back in the dorm and handle your business. The offenders have the stereotype that we don't care {what happens to them}. We are changing that with the younger ones.

Some staff indicated that inmates did not trust staff at the initial reporting phase and inmates, staff felt, doubted staff's ability to follow-up once a report was made.

The specific difficulties in getting attention from outside law enforcement agencies and from local prosecutors was also discussed. As one staff member noted: "I have been on duty during a number of (alleged) incidents. It is tough to deal with; it is tough to get law enforcement to deal with them. In general there is apathy on the part of law enforcement to deal with sexual assaults."

In facilities with cameras, the majority of staff was confident that "this (sexual assault) does not happen here because we have cameras." Others, however, said that staff shortages prevented good use of this equipment.

Staff coverage was identified as a primary way to prevent sexual assaults. Staff shortages, unsafe staff/inmate ratios, and untrained staff were mentioned as contributing to the causes of sexual assault. One respondent indicated "inmates know how long it takes you to count; they time officers on their rounds. They know how much time they have."

Staff identified the following barriers to reporting:

- Inadequate protocols;
- Lack of training on investigation for all staff;
- Inadequate resources to pursue allegations of assault;
- Lack of knowledge about and training on investigation and reporting of inmate prostitution;
- Lack of proper inmate training. Staff stated that inmates very often will not come to them with their concerns and need to be educated that staff is there to help protect from sexual violence;
- The difficulty of determining the degree of coercion among female offenders;
- Lack of follow-up information about assault staff reported;
- Difficulties in prosecuting staff sexual misconduct and inmate-inmate sexual assault; and
- Lack of community awareness on sexual victimization in prisons and jails.

STAFF AND INMATE TRAINING

In about two-thirds of the facilities visited, staff stated that they had little or no training on sexual assault and other forms of violence. In some places, line staff said that supervisors receive the training but they do not. Several reported receiving training on sexual harassment and sexual misconduct, but nothing on inmate-inmate issues. With some exceptions, those who did report receiving training said such training typically focused on investigations, including the collection and preservation of evidence and interviewing victims.

Staff Training

Staff in jails was most likely to receive training on investigations. In a few facilities, participants described on-going staff training on prevention and intervention of sexual assault.

The training emphasis on PREA or whatever comes from the top; line officers notice if the supervisors are committed – they think if the supervisors are not about "it", then I am not about "it" either.

Both the staff who received training and those who desired more training made similar recommendations concerning staff training. They suggested that training should be available to all staff and include information on two primary areas: policy and protocol; and, education and training.

Policy and protocol:

- Agency/facility policy and protocols on responding to sexual assault;

- An emphasis on prevention of sexual assault;

- Reporting and investigation procedures;

- Services and treatment of sexual assault victims, including crisis intervention training;

- Clarifying roles and expectations (custody, mental and physical health, investigation, and supervisors);

- Sanctions regarding perpetrators of sexual assault; and

- Policy and protocol regarding prosecution.

Education and training:

- Staff-inmate rapport, communication and other issues relevant to reporting;

- Understanding of the process of grooming and protective paring, including coerced and consensual relations;

- Characteristics of predatory and vulnerable inmates;

- Histories of sexual abuse;

- Working with female inmates;

- Causes and indicators of potential and completed assault;

- Sensitivity to inmate victims of assaults;

- Cross training across the disciplines and functions of the facility; and

- Use of case study and "real world" scenarios.

Inmate Training

The offenders are coming in younger and younger. Their mentality is that prison is just another part of their life that continues from their neighborhood environment. They don't know what they are going be around here (in prison). They don't know they will be around other criminals that can overpower them with no concern for their feelings or health. The young offenders-the new offenders-have not experienced the brutality of the prison way of life. They have the myth that prison is easy… They need to be told how to protect themselves.

The need for inmate training, education and orientation was mentioned in almost every interview. Staff stated that inmates very often will not come to them with their concerns and need to be educated that staff is there to help protect from sexual violence. Although few facilities currently stressed prevention, almost all staff respondents believed that this would be a productive approach to addressing sexual assault.

Components of inmate education:

- Institutional policy and corresponding sanctions (including agency commitment to addressing sexual assault);

- Awareness of sexual violence, including "red flags" for potential victimization and inmate prevention/protection strategies such as boundaries, coping skills, and the grooming and coercion process;

- The health and safety risks of consensual sexual relations;

- Staff readiness to assist inmates and avenues for reporting both fears and incidents;

- The investigation process (including timeliness and evidence preservation);

- Sanctions for false reporting;

- Warnings to predatory and sexually aggressive inmates; and

- Availability of counseling and other treatment services.

Staff working in women's facilities noted that while some inmate education was available on staff sexual misconduct issues, female inmates should be informed of the specifics of both inmate sexual assault issues and responding to staff sexual misconduct.

Suggestions about forms of all inmate education included: orientation information at intake/reception; videos, peer-based education; presentation by mental health staff; and written materials, pamphlets, posters and the like. Many staff stated that all inmates should receive this information on a recurring basis to re-enforce the seriousness of this issue.

Other suggestions included developing more effective treatment services for inmate victims and identifying safe and private places for inmate to speak with staff. Applying "lessons learned" from community rape prevention programs was also mentioned.

WOMEN'S FACILITIES

Respondents in women's facilities shared many of the perspectives with their colleagues in male facilities. Specific differences included more detailed discussions of the relational context of women's institutions, the rarity of violent sexual attacks, the forms of sexual coercion among female offenders, "touching" and other examples of physical closeness, staff sexual misconduct and concerns over false reports. Staff also mentioned that sexual assault training typically focused on male-based information and that they received very little information about the dynamics and prevention of sexual assault within female facilities. Many staff from mixed or female facilities indicated that they received very little training on working with female inmates in general.

Staff from women's facilities also reported hearing about some sexual intimidation among the women offenders. In general, staff who said that serious violence—sexual or otherwise—was rare in female facilities. Sexual assault takes different forms in female facilities, as this participant noted: "I don't know that there is rape but we do have inappropriate touching among the offenders."

Staff Sexual Misconduct

Staff sexual misconduct involves using power to get what the staff member wants. We are supposed to be taking care of the offenders, not hurting them.

In contrast with the male-based focus group data, the issue of staff sexual misconduct in female institutions was a key element in any discussion of sexual safety and sexual assault. Staff acknowledged that while male staff involvement with female inmates was the more common occurrence, misconduct between female staff and inmates was also a possibility.

The wide majority of the staff indicated a solid understanding of the policies and legal components of staff sexual misconduct. To a person, all correctional staff remarked that sexual interaction of any kind between staff and inmates was "wrong, morally, ethically and legally." One staff member said, "In our position, it is always assault. It can't be consensual even if the inmate gives consent. It does not matter- it is abuse. There is no such thing as willing here."

Although this point of view dominated the data, others suggested that sometimes consensual relationships between staff and inmates were not punished as severely as those defined as willing. Staff also were highly disapproving of other staff who did become involved with inmates sexually, showing a "lack of respect for the profession" and betraying other staff as well.

The safety problem inherent in staff misconduct was discussed in every facility. Staff sexual misconduct was seen as a safety violation and contrary to the purpose of the job itself. Acknowledging that safety is "critical in a female facility," one officer emphasized that any sexual act was seen as "inappropriate" because it is a threat the safety of the facility. Another suggested that staff sexual misconduct stems from staff not really doing their jobs.

The relational aspects of female prison/jail culture are also connected to staff sexual misconduct. Staff in the focus groups also acknowledged that female inmates seek to form relationships with staff. Although some staff felt that misconduct was rooted in predatory individuals, others saw that misconduct was part of a larger problem of inadequate security procedures. This supervisor noted that misconduct occurs "when we are not doing our walks, our checks — it happens when people are not doing their jobs."

The interview participants also explained that female staff can potentially become involved in misconduct, with one staff respondent saying, "It is not just men- there have been female staff involved, too. There have been more women involved than men."

Inmates manipulating or grooming staff for these inappropriate relationships was a key theme in the interviews. Staff also expressed great concern over the validity of claims of staff sexual misconduct and the damage such false accusations could create. Credibility was also an issue in reports of staff sexual misconduct. Staff in every facility was very concerned that co-workers would be damaged by false accusations.

Female Predatory Inmates

Some staff members were uncomfortable with the designation "predatory inmate" when it was applied to female offenders. They acknowledged that some number of women are aggressive in their pursuit of a relationship with other female inmates; this aggression, in turn, may or may not involve coerced sexual acts. Most staff participants described the complexity of defining "predatory behavior" among the women by distinguishing their predations from those normally associated with men:

Like everyone else (in the focus group) I am not aware of violent, sexual rapes and assaults here. We do have predatory inmates who try to take advantage of other inmates.

"Intimidation" was the most often described form of coercion. Typically, as staff described, these coerced acts were most likely to occur in the context of an on-going relationship.

One executive manager in a women's facility stated:

We do not have assaults. No gang activity here. They want one personal friend, not to be part of a group; they have no need for gangs because they are safe here. Things are [not?] about power and control, [but] about safety. Even in the juvenile units [there is] no real gang activity. We try to listen constantly and investigate any negative report.

For those staff participants who work with female populations, the openness of those pursuing a variety of relationships was often described. The difficulty of determining the degree of coercion among female offenders was also detailed in the staff focus groups. The complications of these relationships obscured investigations into possible assaultive relationships.

Female sexual violence between women was defined as being more difficult to detect and prove, as seen in this comment:

It is not like the male inmates, where there is semen; a girl getting touched is harder to prove as opposed to males. [You] have to catch women in the act."

Another staff person described this difficulty by saying, "I don't think there are red flags for women inmates that make them easy to recognize."

Staff also suggested that female inmates were more likely to report abuse than were men. In general, female offenders were seen to be less effected by the "no snitching" rule. It was also suggested that some females were often offended by same-sex behavior and would report it to staff.

Staff perception of female offenders was also grounded in their knowledge of past history of sexual abuse, inappropriate sexualization of women, and other forms of trauma and abuse, as described here:

Women engage in such sexual activity here because of a history of previous abuse and sexual misconduct and are unaware of healthy sexual behavior. Most of the women have been victims; not just in prison, but on the outside also. Most women have been victims and they think that it's okay [to be sexually assaulted or abused].

JAILS

Perspectives of staff from jail settings were parallel to those in the prisons. While these perspectives were largely consistent with those from prison settings, specific differences described in the jail focus group interviews included: the local origin of staff and inmates that affects pre-existing social relationships among these groups; the effect of the shorter incarceration period and the population turnover in the jail on assaults; varying sizes of jail population, as well as design and surveillance issues; and problems related to mixing inmates of different classifications. Jail staff was adamant that training and other information resources designed for prisons were often inappropriate for their facilities.

Specific mention was made of the potential for assault inherent in the "drunk tanks." Intoxicated inmates were seen to be both vulnerable to assault due to their compromised capacity and more likely to assault others because of their disinhibition.

In the jail, overcrowding and staff shortages were seen as critical contributors to the potential for sexual assault:

When you don't have enough staff watching the inmates, inmates can run and do what they please, to a point, and more sexual and physical assaults occur. {Inmates} will hunt out spots where they won't be seen: Shower, bathroom, smoking room that is off to the side. {With our} double cells in the back {we have no coverage} and then you see three or four guys {who are out of bounds} coming out of a cell.

In contrast, one jail participant asserted that due to a design with "wide open places and a lot of officer presence, sexual assault doesn't happen here."

In jails with direct supervision, staff reported success because "the inmates feel safe here. I can't remember the last time a weapon was found in here. It is very safe in here." New generation jails with improved security and technology, such as cameras, were also thought to promote a safer environment. Staff reported that they felt cameras "kept the inmates in check, and videotapes helped clarify issues that came up. They (the inmates) do not know when they are being watched."

Many staff reported that their jail facility had a good classification system and that extensive resources were used to classify inmates properly. The computerized classification system has a "red flag" feature that identifies vulnerable and predatory inmates.

Staff attributed successes in communication to establishing good rapport with inmates, building trust and establishing a presence. The interviews stressed the importance of varying rounds in order to catch inmates off guard; otherwise, inmates can get to know a set schedule. Further, staff noted that teamwork is essential. Staff must cooperate and communicate within and across departments: "I communicate. I have to tell the other officers what happens, so I can work with them, not against them." Others described the "cohesive units formed between the deputy and the medical staff."

In one very large jail, a recent policy change "is more than just hourly checks. It involves interacting with inmates directly-talking to inmates and detecting issues, tension and problems on the floors. This more frequent and direct supervision has had a real impact. Assaults are down in the units. It is more than just extra eyes — while that is a part of it — but the most effective part is talking, interacting with the inmates."

The importance of good policy was illustrated in this comment by a jail administrator:

The staff is clearly aware of the zero tolerance policy and the expectation that they conduct themselves professionally and not abuse their authority toward males or females…we are well aware that there may have been a few gaps that it (policy) could be tweaked or tightened up. The appropriate people are responding to each part of the policy, as we have correctional staff, our medical, and our outside law enforcement support people that play a role. I would say that clear lines are being delineated for who should be doing what.

INVESTIGATIONS

Staff agreed that all reports of sexual violence should be investigated, but also described the barriers to effective investigations. Problems in inmate reporting, changing stories and non-cooperation were among the primary problems identified in the interviews. Some of this reluctance stems from elements of inmate culture, but others suggested it was caused by an inappropriate and uncompassionate approach to inmate interviews. Developing rapport with inmate victims, witnesses and potential predators was mentioned as a critical aspect of investigations. The investigative process was often constrained by confidentiality requirements. In addition to lack of inmate cooperation, staff also described the difficulties in obtaining physical evidence, particularly when reports were not made in a timely manner.

Inadequate protocols and lack of training on investigation for all staff were also mentioned as a barrier to successful investigations. There was no consensus as to the effectiveness of using internal versus external investigators. Many staff believed that outside investigators were not trained to investigate institutional assaults effectively. Inadequate resources to pursue such allegations were frequently mentioned as a problem. Coordination and collaboration among other departments in the facility was mentioned as key components of effective investigations. Conversely, some staff expressed frustration that they were prohibited from obtaining follow-up information about assaults they had reported. Participants of another focus group, which concentrated on Staff Perspectives on Investigations, provided insight on the perspectives and experiences regarding investigation process. The summary of findings will be published in Staff Perspectives, Volume II.

PROSECUTION

There was significant discussion about problems in prosecuting inmate-inmate sexual assaults. Difficulties in prosecuting staff sexual misconduct were also described but much less frequently. In some jurisdictions, strong cooperation existed between the prison or jail facility and the local prosecutor's office. In other places, the respondents felt that the prosecutors office was unwilling to aggressively prosecute inmate assault causes, particularly when the evidence was weak, the inmate victim appeared blameworthy, or there was a lack of interest in prosecuting prison or jail-based cases. This prison manager expresses this point by saying:

The culture in the prosecutors office about prison rape is where corrections was 20 years ago. The community sees that sexual assault is somehow justified. Who cares about inmates when they have probably hurt somebody themselves?

COMMUNITY AWARENESS

Most respondents agreed that the community had little concern over sexual victimization, particularly when the inmate victim was a sex or violent offender. Jokes about sexual assault, such as "don't bend over in the shower in jail," further undermined the public view of this problem. In general, it was suggested, the community needed to be educated about the way corrections works.

STAFF RECOMMENDATIONS

The focus group process also sought recommendations to improve the correctional response to sexual violence.

The recommendations listed below were made in multiple facilities:

- Increasing sanctions for inmate predators;
- Elevating penalties for staff sexual misconduct;
- More direct interaction and visibility with inmates;
- Increasing communication;
  - With inmates;
  - Among all staff members; and
  - With outside investigators and prosecutors.
- Creating an "after-action review" for all sexual assaults incidents;
- Information on "best practices" in responding to sexual assault;
- Implementing a "safe prisons' officer at every facility;
- Developing a centralized and standardized reporting mechanize;
- Enhancing and publicizing avenues of inmate reporting, including "hotlines;" locked suggestion boxes, and outside ombudspersons;
- Improving classification and housing options;
- Creating treatment programs for sex offenders and victims of assault;
- Use of cameras and other emerging technologies (such as "radio frequency" tracking systems);
- Training outside community prosecutors on prison sexual violence; and
- Address leadership and culture.

Suggested Approaches to Responding to Sexual Violence

Prevention and responding to sexual violence in correctional facilities was seen as a form of "good correctional practice." The following components are examples of successful approaches to responding to sexual violence:

Policy:

- "Safe prisons" programs;
- Aggressively promoting a "zero tolerance" policy;
- Emphasizing prevention;
- After-action reviews;
- Collaboration with outside investigators and prosecutors; and
- Investigating all allegations.

Staff development:

- Team work, communication and cooperation;
- Staff awareness and experience;
- Specific training on responding to sexual violence;
- Coordination of all departments (both treatment and investigation); and
- Using inmate advocates;
- Supervisory training; and
- Recognition of warning signs.

Inmate issues:

- Developing rapport and trust with inmates;
- "Walking and talking;"
- Putting inmates on notice;
- Multiple, confidential reporting mechanisms; and
- Referrals to clinical staff.

Housing and classification:

- Direct supervision;
- Single cells;
- Classification system that identifies and separates vulnerable and predatory inmates; and
- Identify isolated areas.

CONCLUSION

This focus group data provide a detailed picture of staff perspectives on sexual violence. As stated in the interviews, responding to sexual assault and other forms of sexual violence is part of good correctional practice. The interviews demonstrate that most staff is knowledgeable about sexual assault and its causes and indicators. The data obtained from these interviews provide a solid evidence base for improving our response to sexual violence by supplying concrete information concerning training and education and policy and protocol development.

Most staff said they had little direct knowledge of sexual assault and other forms of sexual violence. Their information about sexual assault typically was gained after an incident, and came through informal methods (such as discussion with staff or other inmates) or through formal means such as reading investigative reports or briefings, as this example shows:

One day I was off and an inmate got raped with a spoon. I heard about it only. No proof though, inmate victim didn't claim it. Other inmates knew and laughed about it. When you hear about it from another inmate, it's hard to get inmate victims to admit to being raped.

Even though few had direct, personal knowledge most thought that sexual assault occurred more than they knew. Many staff, however, felt that they had a sense of when "something was wrong" and said that they could discern potential or actual sexual abuse incidents by knowing the inmate population, observing predatory behaviors and potential victims.

Direct knowledge of sexual assault was gained primarily through reports from victimized inmates, third-party reporters (including other inmates) and participating in investigatory processes. Staff was concerned about the validity of information they received in the form of gossip and rumor. This was particularly true concerning staff sexual misconduct.

Across the board, staff felt that sexual assault and other forms of sexual violence were relatively infrequent, but most felt that the actual occurrence was difficult to count. Many felt that, while responding to sexual violence was an important part of their job, eliminating sexual assaults within correctional facilities would be extremely difficult.

The next bulletin, Staff Perspectives, Volume II, will focus on staff perspectives on investigations, including barriers to identifying and investigating sexual assault, education and orientation needs, sanctioning, investigative techniques, ways to improve investigative responses to PREA issues, and the next steps.

For more information please contact:

Dee Halley
NIC Program Manager
320 First Street NW, Room 5007
Washington, D.C. 20534
dhalley@bop.gov
1-800-995-6423 ex. 40374

Anadora (Andie) Moss
NIC Project Director
The Moss Group, Inc.
1444 Independence Ave. SE
Washington, D.C. 20003
amoss@mossgroup.us
(202) 546-4747

www.nicic.org